REAL GHOSTS

REAL GHOSTS

Daniel Cohen

Illustrated with photographs and prints

DODD, MEAD & COMPANY
New York

The following illustrations are used by permission and through the courtesy of: John H. Cutten, 51, 53, 70; The Ghost Club, 72; New York Public Library Picture Collection, 19, 35, 63, 80, 110, 113, 115; Photo by Shira, 66; Society for Psychical Research, 14, 48, 61, 64. Photographs on pages 89 and 103 are from drawings by S. Drigin.

Cohen, Daniel.
  Real ghosts.

  Includes index.
  SUMMARY: Accounts of "real" ghost sightings—
some of which have since been proven fraudulent and
some of which have never been satisfactorily
explained.
  1. Ghosts—Juvenile literature. [1. Ghosts]
I. Title.
BF1461.C66   133.1   77-6502
ISBN 0-396-07454-5

For Rupert,
with affection and gratitude

CONTENTS

REAL GHOSTS

DEPOSITED
Beneath this Stone the Mortal Part
of Mrs Susanna Jayne, the amiable Wife of
Mr Peter Jayne, who lived Beloved
and Died Universally Lamented, on
August 8th 1776 in the 45th
Year of her Age.

Skeletons and skulls were often shown on early New England gravestones. They were not meant to represent ghosts. But many people think that is what ghosts look like anyway.

1
MEET THE GHOSTS

What is a ghost supposed to look like?

First you may think of something in a white sheet, with holes for eyes. When you want to dress up as a ghost for Halloween that is the sort of costume you use.

You may think of a ragged figure dragging chains and moaning. Or your idea of a ghost may be a figure you can see through—something that goes in and out of rooms without needing to open the doors.

That is the way ghosts are usually described in stories or shown in movies. But real ghosts come in many different sizes and shapes. Sometimes they are strange and frightening looking. Other times they look very ordinary. It is hard to tell they are ghosts at all. Often ghosts cannot be seen, but are just heard and felt.

This is a book about *real* ghosts.

That needs a little explaining. It does not mean that all of the ghostly events described in this book are true, or that they actually happened just the way they are described. It means that the stories are *supposed* to be true, and at one time a lot of people believed them. People still believe many of them.

There are a lot of ghost stories around that are supposed to be true. There may be an old house nearby that some people say is haunted. Perhaps you know someone who claims that he has seen a ghost. Perhaps you even think you have seen a ghost yourself.

Thousands and thousands of people say they have seen ghosts. Yet most scientists say that ghosts do not exist. After all, the scientists point out, thousands and thousands of people once reported seeing mermaids and unicorns. Mermaids and unicorns definitely do not exist.

At night in the dark we can feel frightened. The wind can sound like the moans of a ghost. The thumping of an open door can become ghostly footsteps. A strange shadow, even a piece of paper carried by a breeze, can look like a ghost. A spooky place like a graveyard can make our imaginations run wild. In short, people make mistakes about ghosts.

Some people lie about them as well. People are always interested in stories about ghosts. The stories are even more interesting when they are supposed to be true. For that reason a lot of "true" ghost stories are just made up.

Scientists are simply not willing to accept ordinary ghost stories. They say better evidence is needed. But there are problems. How do you collect evidence for ghosts? If they exist, ghosts are very hard to pin down. A ghost will not step into a laboratory or parade up a busy street.

About one hundred years ago a group of people in England were troubled by the problem of ghosts. Some of them were scientists. Others were philosophers, writers, historians, or people in other professional fields. They were all intelligent and well-educated and quite serious about ghosts. They decided to try and collect scientific evidence about ghosts. They formed a group called the Society for Psychical Research, or the

Henry Sidgwick, first president of the Society for Psychical Research

SPR. The word "psychical" means things of the spirit.

The SPR still exists today. There are similar groups in other countries, including America, but the one in England is the oldest and most active. That is one of the reasons that so many of the ghosts in this book are from Britain. I don't know whether the British people see more ghosts than people of other lands. But I do know that they have studied them longer and more carefully. The quality of evidence from England is usually better than from other places.

People who study ghosts are called "psychical researchers." A newer term, popular in America, is "parapsychologists." That is a word meaning "studying things *beyond* psychology."

The psychical researchers have not proved their case yet. Most scientists still don't believe in ghosts. Some psychical researchers are not even sure that ghosts exist. They have seen too many mistakes, too many fakes, to be sure of any thing. But they have found many things that they cannot explain. They think that the search for ghosts is worth continuing, no matter what the problems.

Most of the stories in the pages that follow were taken from the files of psychical researchers. They are not just legends or vague tales. They have been checked as far as it is possible to check such stories. Sometimes the checking turned up a mistake, or a fake. Other times the story remained as eerie and puzzling as it did when the investigation first began.

Now let us meet the ghosts!

2

THE BEST GHOST STORY

This is the best real ghost story that I have ever heard.

The strange events took place on December 7, 1918. World War I had just ended. Lieutenant David McConnell was an eighteen-year-old British trainee pilot. He was stationed at a Royal Air Force (RAF) base in a place called Scampton in the English Midlands. On the morning of December 7, his commanding officer asked him to fly a plane to a field at Tadcaster. Tadcaster was about sixty miles northwest of Scampton.

McConnell was to be accompanied by a second pilot in another plane. He was to leave the

plane he flew at Tadcaster and return to Scampton in the second plane. It was a routine mission
for moving a plane from one field to another.

At about 11:30 A.M., shortly before he took off,
McConnell spoke to his roommate, Lieutenant
Larkin. McConnell, Larkin, and a third officer,
Lieutenant Garner Smith, had planned to go out
that evening. McConnell said he had to deliver a
plane to Tadcaster, but he expected to be back
the same afternoon. There was no reason to
change plans.

During the flight to Tadcaster, McConnell and
the second pilot ran into an unexpected heavy
fog. They landed their planes in a field and found
a house with a telephone. They phoned Scampton for instructions. The commanding officer
said they should use their own judgment about
whether to go on or not. So the pair took off
again in the direction of Tadcaster. The fog got
worse. Finally McConnell's companion was
forced to make a landing, but McConnell continued the flight.

He reached Tadcaster safely. A witness at the
field saw his plane make its approach for landing. But the angle of approach was too steep,

18

The type of plane Lieutenant McConnell piloted on his last flight.

and the plane crashed. When witnesses reached the plane they found Lieutenant McConnell dead. He had struck his head on the machine gun mounted in front of the pilot's seat. His watch had also been broken in the crash. It was stopped at exactly 3:25 P.M.

At about the same time that McConnell was killed, Larkin was sitting in the room the two of them shared at Scampton. He was reading a book and smoking. His back was to the door. He heard footsteps coming up the corridor, then he heard the door open and close.

A voice said, "Hello, boy." That was McConnell's usual greeting. Larkin turned and saw McConnell—or what he took to be McConnell—standing in the doorway about eight feet from him. Larkin assumed it was McConnell because of the hat the figure was wearing. McConnell had been in the Naval Air Service before joining the RAF. He was very proud of this. Often he wore a Navy cap instead of the standard flying helmet. The figure in the doorway was wearing a Navy cap.

Larkin, of course, didn't know what had just happened at Tadcaster. He didn't think there was anything odd about his roommate coming in at that moment. He said, "Hello! Back already?" The figure replied, "Yes. Got there all right. Had a good trip." The figure then said, "Well, cheerio!" Then the figure turned and went out, closing the door behind him.

It was a very ordinary scene. Except for one fact. The man Lieutenant Larkin thought he had seen come in the door had just been killed sixty miles away.

A short time later, at 3:45 P.M., Lieutenant Garner Smith entered Larkin's room. He asked about McConnell and said he hoped that he would be back early so the three of them could still go out as planned. Larkin said McConnell was already back. He told Garner Smith that McConnell had come into that very room less than half an hour ago. But we know that McConnell was dead at 3:25. That means that Larkin must have thought he had seen McConnell at almost the exact moment McConnell died.

News of McConnell's death did not reach Scampton immediately. Larkin did not hear of it until early evening when he was eating dinner. An announcement was made over the base loudspeaker. Larkin could hardly believe what he heard. He assumed at first that McConnell had returned to Scampton safely after his mission to Tadcaster. Then he must have taken another plane up. It was during this second flight, Larkin reasoned, that his roommate had been killed.

Only later that evening did Larkin discover the

truth. McConnell had been killed at Tadcaster. He died at almost exactly the moment that he had been "seen" in the room they shared at Scampton.

Larkin told other men on the base of his strange experience. Garner Smith confirmed that he had spoken to Larkin at 3:45 P.M., and had been told that McConnell had entered the room within the last half hour.

A short while later McConnell's family heard about the experience. They wrote to Larkin, asking him what had happened. On December 22, he sent them a letter setting down all the details that he could remember. It was a clear, matter-of-fact letter. Lieutenant Larkin did not believe in ghosts before this experience. He was still skeptical about them afterwards. But he could not explain what had happened. All he could do was insist that things happened the way he said they did.

Eventually the story came to the attention of the Society for Psychical Research. An investigator for the Society talked to Larkin and to

Garner Smith. They stuck to their original stories.

The tale of the "ghost" of Lieutenant David McConnell is a strange one, I'm sure you will agree. But it is not as strange as many other ghost stories. The ghost did not shriek or moan. It did not rattle any chains. It did not warn about things that were going to happen. It did not even look like a ghost. Yet I said this was the best real ghost story that I have ever heard. Why?

The reason is because the evidence is so very good. Many ghost stories are secondhand. They are told by someone who heard it from someone else. But in this case we have an eyewitness account. Everyone who interviewed Lieutenant Larkin found him to be a reliable, honest, and unhysterical young man. He was not the sort of person who normally went around "seeing things." Nothing like that had ever happened to him before.

Another problem with many "real" ghost stories is that they happened a long time before anyone bothered to write them down. Sometimes it is months or years before a person puts down in black and white the details of his ghostly experience. And time plays tricks with the human memory. Even honest people with good memories can make mistakes about details. The longer the period of time between the event and the telling, the more mistakes will be made.

In ghost stories, details are important, in order to establish what really happened. Larkin wrote down his account a little over two weeks after the experience. It would have been better if he had sat down and written it that very night. But he was not interested in psychical research. He did not think his story was ever going to be used as evidence to prove that ghosts exist. He wrote it down only because his dead friend's family asked him to.

As far as ghostly evidence goes a two-week gap is not too bad. The investigators for the SPR also checked Larkin's written account with some of the people he had talked to in the days following December 7. They all agreed that what he had written was just what he had told them. This strengthens the case. Larkin's memory of the event seems excellent.

All the times are well established. There was a

witness to the time McConnell was killed. The dead pilot's smashed watch, stopped at 3:25 P.M., confirms this.

Probably the most important evidence is Garner Smith's visit. Garner Smith did not see McConnell's ghost or whatever it was. He did not see anything unusual. But at 3:45, less than one half hour after the appearance of the figure, he heard the story. At that moment there was no way in which either he or Larkin could possibly have known that their friend was dead. If Larkin had begun talking about seeing McConnell only after he found out that McConnell was dead, the case would not be nearly as good. But he told his story at a time when he had no reason to suspect there was anything strange about it.

Does this mean that we have proof that Lieutenant Larkin saw the ghost of his dead friend? Not necessarily. There are several other possible explanations. Let's take a look at them.

The first possible explanation is that the story is a hoax. Many ghost stories that are supposed to be real turn out to be false. People make them up in order to attract attention, or just to have a good story to tell.

World War I planes

If this account is a hoax, then it could not have been Larkin's alone. Garner Smith would have to be in on it.

Considering everything a hoax does not seem very likely in this case. It would mean that two RAF officers were telling lies about the death of their friend and fellow officer. Many, many RAF men had been killed during the war. Death was not the sort of thing that any of them took lightly.

Even if they had wanted to fool the other men at the base, it would have been downright cruel to tell the story to the dead man's family. But Larkin did tell the story to the family. He told them in writing. Garner Smith later confirmed the story to SPR investigators. We cannot prove that this ghost story was not the result of a hoax. But that explanation does not really seem to fit.

Another possible explanation is mistaken identity. Sometimes people think they have seen the ghost of someone dead. Then it turns out that what they have seen is a living person who resembles the dead person.

Larkin did not see the figure he took to be McConnell for long. It was eight feet away, standing in a doorway. The light was not good. He spoke to the figure and the figure answered. But, if you recall, he never addressed the figure as McConnell. Nor did the figure ever say it was McConnell. Larkin just assumed that it was because it looked like McConnell, and had entered the room he shared with McConnell at about the time he expected McConnell to be there.

The figure was wearing a flight suit. On the

base there must have been dozens of young men about the same age and size as McConnell who might have been wearing flight suits at that time. If one of them had wandered into the room, he might have looked very much like McConnell.

He might have—except for the hat. Remember that McConnell usually wore a Navy cap instead of the usual flight helmet. He was the only man on the base to do that. The figure in the doorway was also wearing a Navy cap. Mistaken identity can be ruled out.

There is another possible explanation. Larkin may have dreamed that he saw McConnell. He insists that he was awake. We know he was awake when Garner Smith came into the room. But we cannot be sure that he did not doze off somewhat earlier. Sometimes people who are sitting quietly can fall asleep without knowing it.

Dreams are strange things. When we dream we are not completely cut off from the outside world. We can hear noises and feel sensations. Sometimes we fit these outside noises and sensations into our dreams. Many people begin to dream of fire engines or police sirens when they hear their alarm clocks ringing in the morning.

Something of the sort may have happened to Lieutenant Larkin.

It might have happened this way. Larkin was sitting in his room and dozed off. In his sleep he heard footsteps, real ones, in the hall. Then he heard a door slam—not his door, but another one in the building. These sounds may have become part of his dream. McConnell had already told him he would be back that afternoon. Larkin may have been anxious for his roommate to come back in time for them to go out that evening. So when he heard the footsteps, and the door slam in his sleep, he may have dreamed that McConnell had returned.

There is no way of proving the experience happened this way. But the explanation is a possible one.

Another possible explanation is that Lieutenant Larkin had a hallucination. That is, he saw something that was not there while he was wide awake. You don't have to be crazy to have hallucinations. They are much more common than most people suspect.

That brings up an interesting question. What is the difference between a hallucination of this sort and a ghost? Larkin was perfectly normal. He did not go around seeing things that were not there all the time. But on this occasion he did see something that was not there, something that could not possibly be there—his dead roommate. Does it make any difference whether we call this figure a hallucination or a ghost? Hallucination sounds more "scientific" and more "realistic," but is it? Psychical researchers often argue over questions like this.

And even if Larkin had been asleep, and the whole thing was a dream, there is still something very strange. Why was he dreaming about McConnell at what may have been the exact moment that McConnell was killed?

Could it be just coincidence? Perhaps it could be. But it is a very strange coincidence.

Now you see why I have called this the best "real" ghost story I ever heard.

3

THE GHOST
AND THE JUDGE

If Lieutenant Larkin's experience is the best ghost story I ever heard, then Sir Edmund Hornby's may be the worst. But it sure sounded good at first. In fact, for a while it looked as if the story provided the kind of proof for the existence of ghosts that psychical researchers had always been looking for. It is a good example of some of the problems they run into.

The first thing that is needed in a report of a ghost is a reliable witness. If someone is known to be a liar, or is insane, and says he has seen a ghost, we do not take him seriously. But there could not have been a more reliable witness than Sir Edmund Hornby.

In 1875, when this event took place, Sir Edmund Hornby was a judge for British interests in the Orient. His title was Chief Judge of the Supreme Consular Court of China and Japan. The court was located in the city of Shanghai, where the judge lived. His was a very important and responsible position.

Everyone wanted to know what the judge's decisions would be. The judgments were announced in the morning. But it was Sir Edmund's practice to write up his judgments the night before. He would then give a copy to the local reporter. In that way the judgments could be printed in the morning paper for everyone to see.

On the night of January 19, the judge wrote out his decision after dinner as usual. He put it in an envelope and gave it to his butler. The butler was told to give the envelope to the reporter when he arrived. The judge then went to bed.

He was awakened by a knocking on his bedroom door. He said, "Come in." The reporter, whom he knew by sight, entered the bedroom. The judge was angry at being awakened. He told the reporter that the butler had the envelope he wanted. But the reporter did not leave. Sir Ed-

A British judge in his robes

mund then noticed that the reporter looked un-
usually pale. The reporter said that he was sorry
for waking the judge up. He had looked for the
judge in his study first, but he was not there. So
he tried the bedroom.

Sir Edmund was really furious now. He again
told the reporter to leave, but again the man
didn't move. The judge was now ready to jump

out of bed and throw the reporter out of his bedroom. But there was something about the reporter's appearance that made him stop. Once again he ordered the man from his room.

Instead of going, the reporter moved toward the bed. He sat down at the foot of the bed. He moved slowly, as if he were in pain. Sir Edmund looked at the clock. The time was twenty minutes past one.

The reporter said, "Time presses." Then he asked the judge for a summary of his decision. He took a small notebook out of his pocket to write it down.

"I will do nothing of the kind," the judge thundered. "Go downstairs and find the butler, and don't disturb me. You will wake my wife. Otherwise I shall have to put you out . . . Who let you in?"

"No one."

"Confound it, what the devil do you mean? Are you drunk?"

"No, and never shall be again," the reporter replied. He then repeated that he wanted the judge's decision. "Time is short."

"You don't seem to care about my time," said

the judge. "This is the last time I will ever allow a reporter into my house."

The reporter's reply stopped the judge short. "This is the last time I shall ever see you anywhere."

The judge was worried now. The reporter was acting so strangely. He was afraid all the noise would awaken his wife who was asleep in the next room. So he decided to give the reporter the summary he had asked for. As Judge Hornby talked, the reporter scribbled quickly in his notebook. Apparently he was taking down the judge's words in shorthand. When the summary was finished the reporter thanked the judge and left. The clock was striking half past one. The strange meeting had taken about ten minutes.

The next morning Judge Hornby received a shock. He heard that the reporter he had talked to had died suddenly that very night. Even more surprising was the time at which the reporter had died.

The reporter had gone to work in his room in the evening. At about midnight his wife came down to ask if he was coming to bed. He said that he only had the judge's decision to get ready. Then he would be finished.

At one-thirty he had still not come to bed. His wife became worried. When she looked in on him she found him dead on the floor. His reporter's notebook lay beside him.

There was writing in the notebook. It said, "In the Supreme Court, before the Chief Judge: The Chief Judge gave judgment this morning in the case to the following effect . . . " This was followed by a few lines of shorthand. But no one could figure out what the shorthand meant.

At an inquest into the reporter's death the doctor estimated that he had died at about one in the morning. The cause of death was a heart attack.

Naturally, Judge Hornby was extremely curious about what had happened. He found out as much as he could. The reporter's wife and servants insisted he had never left the house on the night of his death. The judge's own servants assured him that no one could have come into his own house that night. All the doors and windows had been locked.

The judge only told a few close friends about

his experience. He also talked to his wife about what had happened that night. She seemed to recall hearing her husband talking during the night. But she did not know whom he was talking to or what was said.

Nine years later two British psychical researchers, Edmund Gurney and Frederic Myers, heard about the judge and the ghost. They asked Judge Hornby about it. He dictated the story told here and allowed Gurney and Myers to publish it in one of their books.

Gurney and Myers had spent years collecting accounts of ghostly experiences. They thought this was one of the very best they had ever heard. Sir Edmund Hornby was absolutely sure his account was correct. "As I said then, so I say now—I was not asleep, but wide awake. After a lapse of nine years my memory is quite clear on the subject. I have not the least doubt I saw the man—I have not the least doubt that the conversation took place between us."

It was a perfect ghost story. And all true, too. That's the way it seemed for several months after Gurney and Myers published the details of the case. Then the psychical researchers received a letter from Mr. Frederick H. Balfour. Mr. Balfour was a member of a prominent British family, and a relative of the president of the Society for Psychical Research. Mr. Balfour also knew a good deal about what had happened in Shanghai in January, 1875.

The name of the reporter was not mentioned in the original report. Balfour said it was the Reverend Hugh Lang Nivens, editor of the Shanghai *Courier*. Mr. Nivens, he said, had not died at night, but between eight and nine in the morning, after having a good night's rest.

The judge said that while he was talking to the ghost his wife was asleep in the next room. But the judge was not married at the time of Reverend Nivens' death. His wife had died some two years earlier. The judge remarried, but not until March, 1875, three months after Nivens died.

The judge "remembered" details from the inquest into Reverend Nivens' death. But since Mr. Nivens had died from natural causes, no inquest was ever held.

The "ghost" wanted to get a particular decision that was to be announced on January 20.

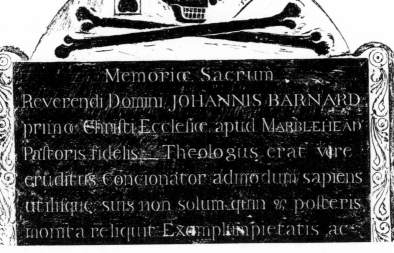

Graveyards can be scary places, particularly with grave-stones like these. But most ghosts are seen in more ordinary surroundings.

The judge gave it to him. The last words in Mr. Nivens' reporter's notebook concerned that decision. That is how Judge Hornby "remembered" the events. But there was no record that any such decision was ever delivered on January 20.

In short, Sir Edmund Hornby's story seemed so full of errors that none of it could be believed. When Judge Hornby saw the Balfour letter he was astonished.

He agreed that his "vision" of the dead reporter must have come some three months after the death, not on the same night. But he still insisted that was not the way that either he or his wife remembered the event. "If I had not believed, as I still believe, every word of it [the story] was accurate, and that my memory was to be relied on, I should not ever have told it as a personal experience."

He certainly would not have. There is no reason to suspect that he made up the story. He had nothing to gain from such a lie. The reputation of a judge who reports seeing ghosts will suffer in any case. Judge Hornby appears to have been a man who made a big, but honest mistake.

42

Could anyone really, honestly, make that big a mistake? The key may be the time. Remember that Sir Edmund Hornby's memories of the event were not written down until nine years after it was supposed to have taken place. He had not even told the story to many people during those years. In that many years his memory of the event could have changed dramatically. What might have started as an ordinary dream about a man who had died, was changed into an encounter with a ghost. Nine years is a long time.

Dreams where the dreamer thinks he has awakened are fairly common. They can be very confusing. You can dream that you woke up and talked to someone, then went back to sleep. When you actually wake up in the morning you may think that you really woke up earlier—not that you just dreamed that you woke up.

Remember in the last chapter I said that it was important to have the details of any ghostly encounter written down as soon as possible. Now you can see why.

4

A SEARCHING GHOST

There are many tales of a ghost that is searching for something. The ghost is seen wandering up and down the halls of a house. It is trying to find something it lost in life. Such tales are more common in fiction than in psychical research. But there is one really good account of a searching ghost.

The haunting began in 1883 and continued for many years. The haunted house was a large pleasant house in the Cheltenham section of London. The house was called Garden Reach. The case is usually called the "Cheltenham Haunting."

The main witness to the haunting was Miss

Rosina Despard. She was in her early twenties at the time. She wrote a very clear account of what she had seen for the Society for Psychical Research. She also cooperated fully with Society investigators. Later, Miss Despard went to medical school and became a doctor. During her medical career she held several important positions. It was unusual for a woman even to become a doctor in those days. She was a very strong and intelligent woman, and thus a very good witness.

Rosina's father, Captain F.W. Despard, and his family moved into the house in April, 1882. It wasn't until the following June that Rosina first saw the ghost.

She was in her room one night when she heard something at the door. She opened the door, but no one was there. Then she saw the figure of a tall lady walking through the hall. The figure went down the stairs, and Miss Despard followed it. However, she only had a small candle and it went out. Not being able to see anything else, she went back to her room.

Later, Miss Despard saw the ghost again and got a better look at it. The figure was wearing a black woolen dress. The face was hidden by a handkerchief held in the right hand. The lady seemed to be wearing a bonnet with a long veil or hood. The outfit looked like one that would be worn by a widow.

Miss Despard was not at all afraid of the ghost. She was just curious about it. She followed it when she could. One time she cornered it and tried to touch it, but it got away. She tried to speak to it, but it would not answer. One time, though, it gave "a slight gasp." Miss Despard thought that the figure couldn't speak.

On two occasions Miss Despard hung strings in the hall where the ghost often walked. She saw the ghost pass right through the strings without moving them. She also tried to take a picture of the ghost, but the light was never good enough. Miss Despard kept a careful record of all her encounters with the ghost. Her account of the haunting was published by the Society for Psychical Research.

The ghost was usually seen in the house, and only for brief periods. But occasionally it was seen in the garden. Once Miss Despard was able to watch it for nearly half an hour.

Frederic Myers, who investigated the "Cheltenham Haunting"

Other people saw the ghost too. Frederic Myers, an investigator for the Society for Psychical Research interviewed six others who claimed to have seen the ghostly figure at least once. There were several others who also were supposed to have seen it, but Myers was not able to talk to them.

Not everybody in the house saw the ghost, however. Captain Despard and his wife never saw it, though they lived in the house. On several occasions Miss Despard saw the ghost enter the room where her father or other members of her family were sitting. She pointed the ghost out to them, for she could see it quite clearly. She was astonished to find that they saw nothing.

While not everyone saw the ghost, most people who stayed in the house reported hearing ghostly footsteps. Miss Despard said that the footsteps were not like those of any living person in the house. "They are soft and rather slow, though decided and even." Her sisters and the servants would not go out of their rooms when they heard the footsteps pass. But she did, and every time she saw the ghostly figure.

The haunting was at its height between 1884

and 1886. In additon to the footsteps, there were all sorts of unexplained loud noises heard in those years.

After 1886, the figure was seen much less frequently. It seemed to be quite literally fading away. At first it appeared very solid and lifelike, but later it was less distinct. Footsteps were still heard occasionally. After 1891, there were no further reports of the ghost at Garden Reach.

Miss Despard tried to identify the ghost. The most likely candidate seemed to be Imogen Swinhoe. Garden Reach was built in 1860. The first occupant was Henry Swinhoe. His first wife died in the house, and then he married Imogen.

There is some argument about what sort of person Imogen Swinhoe was. According to Miss Despard's story, Henry Swinhoe had taken to drink after his first wife's death. His second wife tried to cure him, but failed. Instead, she took to drinking herself.

But the descendants of Henry Swinhoe's first wife tell a different story. They say it was Imogen who had been the heavy drinker, and she drove her husband to drink.

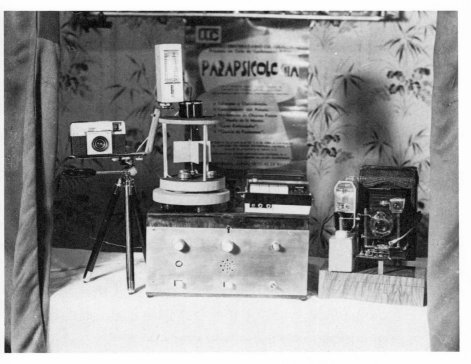

A "ghost detection device." Any sort of disturbance, like noise or vibration, will set off the automatic camera.

Whatever the case, it was not a happy marriage. There were constant quarrels and violent scenes. The children hated their stepmother, whom they considered a cruel tyrant.

Imogen Swinhoe left her husband in 1875. A few months later Henry Swinhoe died, and the children went to live with a guardian. Imogen

Swinhoe died on September 23, 1878. She had never returned to Garden Reach.

Since the ghost Miss Despard had seen was apparently a widow, and Imogen Swinhoe was the only widow associated with the house, she was an obvious candidate. But she did not die at Garden Reach. Why should she be haunting it?

Miss Despard assumed that the ghost of the second Mrs. Swinhoe was looking for the first wife's jewels. Miss Despard heard that a carpenter who had worked for Henry Swinhoe had built a special secret hiding place under the floor of one of the rooms. The carpenter said that the hiding place was for the first wife's jewels, so that Imogen could not find them.

Captain Despard had the floor boards torn up. The hiding place was found, but it was empty.

No one seemed to know what had happened to the jewels. Swinhoe family papers referred to "original jewels." They were supposed to have been taken from the house by Henry Swinhoe and deposited in a bank, but no record of the deposit was ever found.

Miss Despard never saw a picture of Imogen Swinhoe. Once she did pick out a picture of

This is what many people think that ghosts are supposed to look like. This photograph, however, is a fake.

Imogen's sister, and said that it looked like the ghost she had seen. Imogen was reported to resemble her sister very much. Several people who had known Imogen also identified her from

Miss Despard's description.

Still, psychical researcher Frederic Myers was careful. "The evidence for the identity of [the ghost] is inconclusive," he wrote.

For a long time the Cheltenham ghost was very famous. Myers called it "one of the most remarkable and best authenticated on record." But after the ghost had not been seen for many years people stopped talking about it. The house was eventually sold to a church group. It was renamed St. Anne's. No one who stayed in the house was troubled by ghosts. In fact, very few knew the house was ever supposed to have been haunted at all.

Then, in the 1970s, the old "Cheltenham Haunting" became the object of interest to psychical researchers once again. Researcher and writer Andrew MacKenzie heard that in 1958 and again in 1961 the strange figure was seen again. It was not seen in the house where it first appeared, but at another house in the neighborhood.

In October, 1958, a man named John Thorne who lived near the old haunted house had an odd experience. He woke up in the middle of the night to find a strange woman in his bedroom. It was dark and he could not see her very well. But he could make out that she was wearing a long dress, the kind people wore a hundred years ago. Thorne woke up his wife, who turned on the lights. The figure disappeared. His wife told him he was dreaming and should go back to sleep.

Thorne was embarrassed. He told no one about his experience. His wife said she did not repeat the story either. In 1961, John Thorne's brother William and his family came for a visit. William and his teen-aged son were sharing a room.

On the first night William Thorne heard footsteps outside the door. When he looked out of the open door he saw a woman in a long black dress. She was holding a handkerchief up to her face so he could not see it clearly. She had the handkerchief in her right hand. Thorne's son also saw the figure. They remembered that the room suddenly seemed to become very cold.

When William told his brother what had happened, John Thorne replied, "Thank God. I thought I had been dreaming." He then told his brother about the woman he had seen in 1958.

Years later William Thorne ran across a magazine article about the original "Cheltenham Haunting." The ghost sounded exactly like what he had seen. He particularly noticed the feature about the handkerchief being held to the face. He contacted Andrew MacKenzie. Both William and John Thorne made sworn statements as to what they had seen. Both insisted that they had never heard of the "Cheltenham Haunting" before they had their strange experiences.

The Thorne evidence is not nearly as impressive as the original account by Miss Despard. Both men could have been dreaming, though they insist they were awake. It is also possible that both men could have heard of the "Cheltenham Haunting" at some earlier time. They might have forgotten about it consciously. But the memory might still have been buried in their minds, and come out in a dream. There is really no way of knowing.

Still, the coincidence—if that's what it is—is a strange and spooky one. It adds a modern touch to what had been called one of the best authenticated ghost stories of the last century.

5

GHOSTS ON FILM

For a long time now people have been trying to prove that ghosts are real. It has not been an easy job. Most of the evidence for ghosts comes from people who said they saw one. But people can tell lies and make mistakes. We know that.

A photograph of a ghost would be a more solid piece of evidence. But taking a picture of a ghost is a difficult task. Rosina Despard tried to photograph her ghost without success. Still, there have been a lot of photographs that were supposed to show ghosts. Most of these photographs have not been very convincing. There are a few, however, that have been really puzzling and mysterious.

People began trying to take pictures of ghosts from the time photography first developed. But in the early days photography was crude. Most people did not understand it very well and they made mistakes.

A classic mistake was almost made by Frank Podmore, one of the best of the early psychical researchers in Britain. Podmore was shown a picture of the inside of an English chapel. In the picture was the faint, ghostly outline of a human face.

The photographer said that he was taking a picture of the chapel. Nothing unusual happened during the picture taking. Only after the film was developed did he see the human face. Then he recognized the face as that of a young friend who had recently died a tragic death.

Podmore, who had seen lots of fakes, was impressed. He thought the man was honest. "When he told me the story and showed me the picture, I could easily see the faint but well-marked features of a handsome, melancholy lad of eighteen."

Podmore did not stop there. He showed the picture to someone else, but did not tell the story of the dead boy. This person identified the face as that of a woman about thirty. Podmore decided that "The outlines are in reality so indistinct as to leave ample room for the imagination to work in."

But whether a boy of eighteen or a woman of thirty, there did seem to be a ghostly face in the picture. How did it get there? The answer lies in the way photographs were taken many years ago. It took a long time to take a picture. This was particularly true if the light was not bright. The inside of a chapel would not be well lighted. Such a photograph could take an hour or more. The photographer would set up his camera on a three-legged stand called a tripod. He would expose the film, then walk away. It could take as long as an hour for the image to register on the film.

During that period someone might walk into the range of the camera. He might even stare at the camera for a few seconds. Cameras were unusual in the early days, and people were curious about them. The image of the intruder would register lightly on the film. When the picture was developed it would appear faint and "ghostly." If the photographer did not know that someone had walked into his picture, he might think he had photographed a ghost. Today, cameras are much better. Pictures are taken in a fraction of a second. Such mistakes are not made anymore.

Many of the early ghost pictures were not mistakes at all. They were deliberate fakes. Some professional photographers would take a picture of a person in their studios. When the picture was developed, what appeared to be a ghostly figure was standing behind or alongside the living person. Usually this figure was identified as a dead friend or relative. These so-called "spirit photographs" often cost a lot of money.

They were all fakes. There were several ways of making them. The most popular was to first take a picture of the subject. Later, after the subject had left, the film was quickly exposed again to get the spirit in it. The "spirit" was usually the photographer's assistant wrapped

An early "spirit photograph"

up in white cloth so he could not be recognized. Some "spirit photographers" even used a dummy draped in cloth.

A riskier, but quicker, way was to photograph the subject and spirit at one time. In early photography the subject had to sit very still, without moving for several minutes. During that time the "spirit" sneaked up quietly behind and posed for a few seconds. On the final picture the outline of the "spirit" would be vague and appropriately ghostly.

For years "spirit photography" was popular in many parts of the world. In 1875, a fake spirit photographer was arrested by the police in Paris. At his trial he freely admitted that he had faked his pictures. The dummy he had used as his "spirit" was shown at the trial. But many of those who had bought spirit photographs from him refused to believe that the pictures had been faked. They were absolutely sure that the "spirit" in their photograph was really that of a dead friend or relative. No matter how many times the fake spirit photographer confessed what he had done, they would not believe him.

How "spirit photographs" can be faked. A photographer's assistant, dressed as a spirit, could sneak up behind the subject.

Another early-day "spirit photograph"

They wanted to believe that the photographs were real. In the face of all evidence, they did.

Spirit photography is no longer popular today. It hasn't been for a long time. When we look at some of the old spirit photographs we wonder how anyone could have been fooled by them. But many years ago people didn't know much about photography. It seemed almost magical. There was a saying, "The camera doesn't lie." Now we know that the camera can be made to lie.

But there are a couple of ghost pictures which cannot easily be brushed aside as mistakes or fakes. For example, there is the picture of the "Brown Lady" of Raynham Hall. The "Brown Lady" is just one of a huge flock of ghostly figures that have been reported walking the halls of old English castles and mansions. But the "Brown Lady" is different in one way—she is the only one who ever had her picture taken.

Raynham Hall is a large stately home in Norfolk, England. It was owned by the Townshend family. The ghostly figure was first seen there

The "Brown Lady" of Raynham Hall

during the Christmas season, 1835. One of the guests who had come down for Christmas was a Colonel Loftus. He was going up to his room when he saw a strangely dressed woman in the hall. He adjusted his glasses to try and get a better look at her. As he did, she disappeared.

A week later Colonel Loftus saw the figure again. In fact, he nearly ran into her. He described her as being a noble-looking lady wearing a brown satin dress. Her face seemed lit by an unearthly light. But the strangest thing about her was that she had no eyes—only empty sockets where the eyes should have been. She was not a pleasant sight.

When Colonel Loftus told his story, some people laughed. Others did not. They reported that they, too, had seen the strange figure. Colonel Loftus drew a sketch of the woman he had seen. An artist made a painting from the sketch. The painting called "The Brown Lady" was hung in a room where the figure had been seen.

Some years later the writer, Captain Frederick Marryat, was staying at Raynham Hall. He thought the stories about the ghost were nonsense. He asked to sleep in the "haunted room"

67

where the portrait of "The Brown Lady" was hung. He spent some time examining the evil-looking figure in the portrait.

Later that evening Marryat and two companions were walking along an upstairs corridor. They saw the figure of a woman carrying a lamp coming toward them. They hid behind a door, as the figure approached, soundlessly. Light from the lamp reflected off the brown dress. As she passed the door she turned her eyeless face toward them and grinned in a "diabolical manner."

Captain Marryat happened to be carrying pistols at the time. He jumped from behind the door and fired point blank at the figure. If someone had been trying to play a joke on him it would have turned out badly indeed. But the bullets passed right through the figure, which immediately disappeared.

The "Brown Lady" was not reported again until 1926, when it was seen by two boys. But it was what happened in 1936 that made this ghost so famous. On September 19, two photographers from the magazine *Country Life* arrived at

Raynham Hall. They were supposed to take pictures of the inside of the house.

One of the photographers, Captain Provand, had just taken a picture of the ancient staircase of the house, and was getting ready to take another. While Captain Provand was leaning over his camera, putting in a new plate, the other photographer, Mr. Indre Shira, stood holding the flash gun. Suddenly he shouted that he could see a shadowy form on the stairs. It looked like a woman draped in a veil.

As the figure glided toward the photographers, Shira told Provand to take another shot immediately. Provand was still leaning over his camera and never saw the figure. But he took the picture.

When the photograph was developed it showed a dim and ghostly-looking figure on the stairs. You could not make out any features. When the photo was first published in *Country Life* on December 16, 1936, it attracted a lot of attention. Several photography experts went to the *Country Life* offices to examine the original negative. They said the picture did not look as if it had been faked. But we cannot be sure. Nor

can we be sure whether the "ghost" is just some smoke, or the result of a fault in the camera or film. But the picture is still considered one of the best and most puzzling of ghost photographs.

The puzzle is still there. Unfortunately, the "Brown Lady" of Raynham Hall has not been photographed or even seen since 1936.

Even more striking and puzzling is a picture taken in 1966. Two Canadians—the Reverend Ralph Hardy, a retired clergyman, and his wife— were visiting the National Maritime Museum in Greenwich, England. One of the buildings on the museum grounds is the Queen's House. It was built for Anne of Denmark, wife of King James I of England.

The Queen's House has a fine spiral staircase, called the Tulip Staircase. It attracted Reverend Hardy's attention. He decided to take a picture of it. The staircase looked empty when the shot was taken.

The figure (or figures) on the Tulip Staircase

After Reverend Hardy returned to Canada and developed the picture, he found it contained a surprise. What looked like a robed figure was climbing the staircase. His (her?) left hand with a ring on it was clearly seen holding the hand rail.

Some people think they can see a second or even a third robed figure in the picture. The original photograph was in color. It is difficult to see the other figures in a black and white reproduction.

The Reverend Mr. Hardy and his wife were not at all interested in ghosts. But they did send the picture to psychical researchers in London. It was examined by photograph experts who said they could not find any evidence of trickery. The Hardys were also interviewed by psychical researchers. The researchers were convinced that the Canadian couple had no reason for taking a fake ghost photograph.

An odd thing about the picture is that the Queen's House and its Tulip Staircase never had any reputation for being haunted. After the photograph became known, some people said they too had seen ghostly figures in or near the Queen's House. But such stories were not taken seriously.

A group called the London Ghost Club organized an all-night vigil at the Queen's House. They set up several scientific instruments, including automatic cameras and recorders. The

Participants in a televised ghost hunt were (left to right) Stringer Davis, actress Margaret Rutherford, and medium Tom Corbett.

results were disappointing. There were a few unexplained noises. But there always are in old houses. They found nothing that could explain the photograph in any way.

The picture of the robed figures on the Tulip Staircase remains a mystery. Some think it may be the best ghost picture ever taken.

The photograph of the "Brown Lady" and the figures on the Tulip Staircase were not taken by people who had set out to photograph a ghost. People who set out to photograph ghosts have been less successful. Many psychical researchers have spent nights sitting around drafty castles or old houses, waiting for ghosts to appear. Usually the ghosts have disappointed them.

An NBC television crew set up an automatic camera in Longleat Manor in England, which was supposed to be haunted. The camera did capture a faint unexplained glow on the stairs. The picture was part of a television special on ghosts during the 1960s. The show was called "The Stately Ghosts of England." The NBC picture was not nearly as impressive a picture as the "Brown Lady" or the Tulip Staircase photograph. Ghosts, if they exist, are not anxious to be on television.

6

THE MOST
FAMOUS GHOST

To tell the truth, most ghosts don't have much of a personality. They seem vague and distant. Often they don't even have a name. But there is one ghost who was very solid. And she had a very definite personality. Her name was Katie King. She has every right to be called the most famous ghost in the world.

Katie came from a long line of ghosts. The first of her ghostly family to appear on earth was her brother, John King. According to some accounts, John King was her father. But that doesn't make any difference.

John had been a pirate in life, the terror of the

Portrait of the ghost, John King.

Spanish Main, to hear him tell it. Even as a spirit he was pretty lively. He often swore. Some people found his language shocking. Usually Katie was different. She was a very gentle spirit.

John and Katie King made their first appearance in 1852 in a log cabin in Athens County,

Ohio. The cabin was owned by Jonathan Koons. It was said to be the scene of many strange and ghostly happenings.

Jonathan Koons said he was a "medium." A medium is a person who is supposed to be able to reach the spirits of the dead. People gather together with a medium for what is called a "séance." During the séance the spirits are supposed to talk or to move objects. Sometimes they even appear in the room. When they do, that is called a "materialization."

The spirits at Koons' log cabin were very active. One night they staged a full-scale concert. " . . . the fiddle, drums, guitar, banjo, accordion, French harp, tea bell, triangle, etc. played their parts." That is what someone who attended the event wrote.

John and Katie King were often heard from. There were sixty-five other King spirits. They all claimed to be John King's ancestors.

Naturally, these spirit activities attracted a lot of attention. Many people wanted to get inside Koons' cabin to see and hear what was going on. Koons charged admission. That may give you a clue to what was really going on.

Katie King as she is said to have appeared at a séance in Philadelphia.

Jonathan Koons was a fake. All of the voices, and noises, and everything else were faked. He was out to make money, and he did—for a while. But he was not a very good fake. People soon caught on to what he was doing. They would no longer pay to attend his spirit "performances."

Jonathan Koons wasn't the only fake medium. There were lots of them. Some were much better than Koons. One of the best was an Italian woman named Eusapia Palladino. Eusapia began her career in the city of Naples in Italy. But she become so well known that she traveled throughout the world. She visited America several times and was very popular.

She was also investigated by many psychical researchers. Some of them thought she really could get in touch with the spirits. But most of them thought she was a fraud. During one séance in America, a ghostly guitar was heard playing. Eusapia claimed it was being played by the spirits.

But, unknown to Eusapia, an investigator all dressed in black slipped into the darkened room. He crawled under the table at which Eusapia sat. Then he saw what was happening. Eusapia was playing the guitar with her toes. He grabbed her by the foot and she screamed. The séance was over.

John and Katie King were frequently reported at Eusapia's séances. Notes "signed" by them often appeared "mysteriously" in the room. Eusapia had probably never heard of Jonathan Koons. All she knew was that the Kings were popular spirits with other mediums, so she adopted them.

Without a doubt Katie King's most spectacular appearances came at the séances of a young English medium named Florence Cook. During Florence Cook's séances she would go into a

The medium Eusapia Palladino

cabinet that was closed off by a curtain. Sometimes a whole room was curtained off to serve as a cabinet. There she was supposed to go into a trance. Out of the cabinet would step Katie King. The "spirit" would walk around the room, talk to people, even touch them. The room was pretty dark. But, still, some people remarked that it was amazing how much Florence Cook resembled the spirit of Katie King. In fact, Katie King looked just like Florence Cook wearing a veil.

In order to show people that she did not just dress up as the spirit of Katie King, Florence Cook would let someone tie her to a chair in the cabinet. Then the curtains would be closed. In a few moments Katie King would step out. When the séance was over, the curtains would be opened. Florence Cook would be found still tied to her chair.

But everyone was not convinced. No one had ever seen the medium and the spirit at the same time. Some said that the medium slipped out of the ropes and put on her Katie King outfit. Then she was able to slip back into the ropes after the performance was over. Professional magicians were able to do that sort of thing.

Look-alikes; medium Florence Cook and the "spirit" of Katie that appeared at her séances.

At one séance there was a man named W. Volckman in the group. Volckman had been sent by a rival medium. He was out to make a fool of Florence Cook. While Katie was walking around, Volckman grabbed her. He was trying to prove that the spirit was only Florence in disguise. Katie slapped Volckman, scratched him, and swore loudly at him.

Then all the lights went off. The people bumped into one another. No one knew what was happening. In the confusion the spirit of Katie King escaped from Volckman's grasp. When the lights went on again Florence Cook was found in her cabinet. She was still tied to her chair.

Word of this incident got around. It hurt Florence Cook's reputation. She decided that she had to have someone verify her powers as a medium. She chose William Crookes to do the investigating.

William Crookes was a very important man. He was a scientist of the first rank. His discoveries are still discussed in modern textbooks. He had been interested in psychical research for years. Most other scientists thought he was wasting his time, but they still recognized his brilliance. They even elected him the president of the Royal Society, the most important scientific society in Britain. Even today the name of William Crookes would still appear on any list of top scientists who ever lived. He was particularly well known for his careful laboratory work.

Crookes' interest in mediums was well known. He took up the task of investigating Florence Cook with enthusiasm. In one set of tests he used equipment dreamed up by an electrician named Cromwell Valery. The tests took place in 1874.

Thin wires were attached to the medium's arms and shoulders while she sat in her cabinet. These led to a device outside the cabinet, in plain view of the experimenters. The device would register if the medium even moved her arms. It would go wild if she tried to get out of her chair or take off the wires.

The séance went on as usual. During the first half hour the instrument registered only minor changes. This must have been due to Florence shifting in her chair. Then the spirit of Katie King peered out from the curtains.

A few minutes later she was walking around the room. She put her hand on Crookes' head. She took a paper and pencil and wrote some messages. All of this time the instrument registered no change at all. The spirit went back to the cabinet. When the curtains were opened the medium was found with the wires still attached to her.

That sounds like pretty conclusive proof. But it isn't really. All scientific experiments should be described carefully in writing. In this way other scientists can try and repeat them to see if they get the same results. The experiments with Florence Cook were written up, but very badly. Frank Podmore, the psychical researcher, read the record. He complained that there was really no way of telling what had gone on. Modern attempts to repeat the experiment have failed. The electrical equipment that Crookes describes cannot be made to work properly.

Many people have said that Crookes could have been fooled. Professional magicians, whose business it is to fool people, have been very critical of Crookes. One magician, J.N. Maskelyne, said, "As a believer, Mr. Crookes is

all very well; as an investigator, he is a failure."
The celebrated Harry Houdini was even more
critical. "There is not the slightest doubt in my
mind that this brainy man was hoodwinked . . . "
Houdini had investigated many mediums. He
thought they were all frauds.

But Crookes did more than attach wires to
Miss Cook, and look at dials. During one séance
he actually went "into the cabinet" with her. The
"cabinet" in this case was a room in Crookes'
own house that was curtained off. No one else in
the séance group could see what was going on
inside.

Crookes said that in the cabinet he talked with
the spirit of Katie King. He then walked across
the room to where he saw the medium lying on
the floor. This was the key test. Crookes said he
saw the medium and the spirit at the same time.
Crookes' description of the remarkable meeting
continues:

"Stooping over her, Katie touched her, and
said, 'Wake up, Florrie, wake up! I must leave
you now!' Miss Cook then woke and tearfully
entreated Katie to stay a little time longer. 'My
dear, I can't; my work is done. God bless you,'

William Crookes said he saw both the spirit of Katie and the medium at the same time.

Katie replied . . . Following Katie's instructions, I then came forward to support Miss Cook, who was falling onto the floor, sobbing hysterically. I looked around, but the white-robed Katie had gone."

A clever faker might have found some way to fix the electrical device used by Crookes. But it does not seem possible that Sir William Crookes could have been fooled when he entered the cabinet with Katie and saw the medium on the floor. Miss Cook might have had an accomplice who played the part of the spirit. But the accomplice could not have gotten in and out of the room without being seen by others.

There is also the possibility that Florence Cook really *could* contact the dead. And that the spirit of Katie King, who appeared at her séances, was a real ghost. But this is hard to believe. For years psychical researchers tested mediums like Florence Cook. They all turned out to be fakers. Miss Cook herself was caught faking on several occasions.

A third possibility is that Florence Cook was a fake, and the distinguished scientist William Crookes was helping her cheat. A lot of people thought so at the time, and said so. Crookes always denied it. But he was never able to produce any other evidence of the existence of the spirit of Katie King either.

For a while some people thought that Crookes' testimony was the best evidence for the existence of spirits of the dead. But as time went on, even those who had once been convinced began to have doubts about what had happened. Finally, people just stopped talking about Florence Cook and William Crookes.

In 1962, the old case came up again. A psychical researcher named Trevor H. Hall looked over all the evidence he could find. He came to the conclusion that the medium Florence Cook and the scientist had indeed been liars. The reason, said Hall, was that Crookes was in love with the pretty young medium. The "séances" were really just an excuse for the two of them meeting. Hall found evidence that before she died Florence Cook admitted she had been a fake.

Some people still think William Crookes had the last word. According to a modern medium,

Grace Rosher of London, she was contacted by the spirit of the long-dead Crookes after Trevor Hall wrote a book about his theory. The spirit denied the whole thing. "I cannot imagine how such an absurd suggestion could be made," the spirit of William Crookes said.

Psychical researchers do not really take the Crookes-Cook episode as serious evidence anymore. Still, it remains one of the strangest stories in the history of research about ghosts.

7

THE REAL EXORCIST AND OTHERS

The Exorcist was an extremely popular book. It was about a young girl who was "possessed" by the devil. It took a ritual called "exorcism" to drive out the evil spirit. An even more popular movie was made from the book. Many people thought that the book and the movie were true.

They were not. The book was a piece of fiction written by William P. Blatty. But Blatty's book was based on a real case. One of the reasons that the book and the movie were so popular is that people thought they were actually a real case. Here we have to be very careful. "Based

93

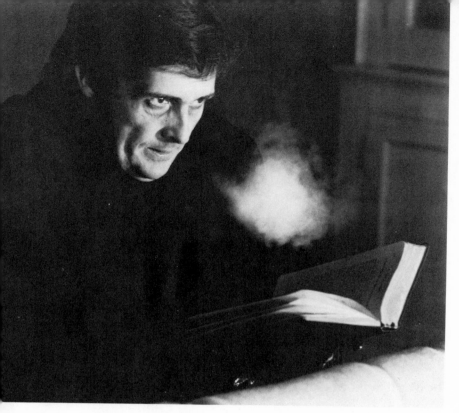

Scenes from the movie "The Exorcist"

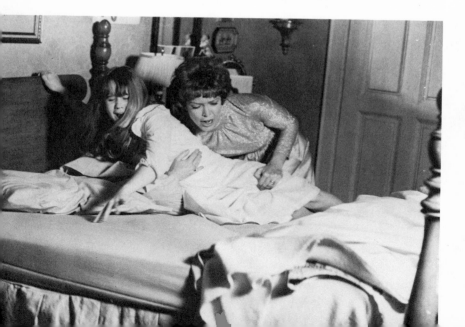

on" is not "the same as." The writer and the movie producers made many changes in order to make *The Exorcist* more dramatic and exciting than the case that inspired it.

In the book and movie the "possessed" subject was a girl. In the real case it was a boy. And that was just one of the changes made. There were many many more.

A large part of *The Exorcist* was not based on anything at all. It was just made up. One reason is that we don't really know a great deal about the real case. Very few records were kept. Not all of what few there were have been made public. Some of those involved in the case have since died. Many others just don't want to talk about it anymore.

Here is what we do know. The case began early in 1949. The possessed subject was a fourteen-year-old boy who has been called Douglas Deen. He lived with his family in a suburb of Washington, D.C.

The first thing the family noticed was strange noises coming from the boy's room. They suspected mice. Exterminators were called in but found nothing. And the noises continued.

The disturbances became more violent. Heavy furniture moved back and forth. A bowl fell off the top of the refrigerator for no apparent reason. A picture seemed to jump off the wall. The worst disturbances took place in the boy's bedroom. His bed shook and trembled all night long. The noise kept Douglas and his parents awake night after night.

The Deens talked about the events with their neighbors. The neighbors laughed at first. But after they spent a night in the Deen house they stopped laughing. The neighbors also began to believe that something very strange was going on. But what?

The Deen family then called in the minister of their church, the Reverend Mr. Winston. The minister, too, was skeptical. But he decided to investigate more closely. He spent the entire night of February 17, 1949, in Douglas Deen's bedroom. Later, the Reverend Mr. Winston described what happened that night to a meeting of the Society for Parapsychology in Washington.

First, the boy's bed began to shake. Then there were scratchings and scrapings from the wall. The minister switched on the light, but could see nothing that might be causing the disturbances.

The minister then asked the boy to sit in an armchair. The chair began to move around the room slowly. Then it started rocking back and forth. Finally it tipped over, throwing the boy on the floor.

Reverend Winston thought it would be best to get the boy out of the furniture which seemed to move. He told the boy to take his pillow and blankets and sleep on the floor. While Reverend Winston watched, the boy and the bedding began to slide across the room. Reverend Winston was then convinced that something very odd was going on. But he did not know what. He felt that the events were beyond his understanding and control.

The boy was taken to Georgetown hospital for both physical and mental tests. The tests turned up nothing. Visits to a psychiatrist did not make the disturbances that centered around the fourteen-year-old disappear.

The Deen family became desperate. They finally decided on a drastic cure. They called in a priest to perform an "exorcism." Exorcism is a very old ritual. Its purpose is to drive out demons. It is not used very often in the modern world. Many people do not approve of using it at all. But the family did not know where else to turn. They believed that exorcism was their last hope.

The priest who performed the exorcism remained with the boy for over two months. During the period he performed the long exorcism rite thirty times. While the ritual was going on the boy would tremble violently. Sometimes he would begin to scream. Then the voice was not at all like his normal voice.

In May, 1949, the priest went through the entire ritual again. The boy did not react violently as he usually did. The priest assumed that the demon had been driven out. After that the boy was no longer troubled by shaking beds or moving furniture.

What does all of this have to do with ghosts? Perhaps a great deal. Psychical researchers found the details of this case very familiar. The unexplained noises, the shaking furniture, and the rest of the things that happened to the Deen boy had troubled many others. Usually these disturbances were not blamed on demons. They were said to be due to the activities of a poltergeist. "Poltergeist" is a German word. It means "noisy ghost" or "noisy spirit."

When we speak of a ghost we usually mean that someone sees the figure of a dead person. But in a poltergeist case people don't usually see any figures at all. What happens is just what happened in the Deen case. There are all sorts of unexplained disturbances in a house. Often these disturbances are blamed on an unseen spirit—a poltergeist.

Hundreds of poltergeist cases can be found in the records of different psychical research organizations. Reports of such experiences go back to ancient times. New ones are reported every year.

Usually psychical researchers hear about a case after it is over, that is, after the disturbances have stopped. But occasionally they are able to investigate while the disturbances are still going on.

That happened in 1958. We like to think of ghosts or spirits haunting crumbling castles or ancient houses. This ghost (if that's what it was) began causing trouble in a modern ranch house. The house was located in the very ordinary suburban community of Seaford, Long Island.

In the house lived Mr. and Mrs. James Hermann and their two children. The children were a girl Lucille, thirteen, and a boy Jimmy, twelve. Most of the disturbances seemed to center around the boy. When he was around things began to happen.

The disturbances began on February 3. First, the family heard what sounded like popping bottles. When they went to see what was wrong, they found bottles in several parts of the house had been mysteriously opened and spilled. A few small objects had also been broken.

Strange noises and bottle openings continued for three days. The family became very concerned. They called the police. Patrolman J. Hughes came to the house. He too heard some noise. He looked in the bathroom and found that some medicine and shampoo bottles had been opened and spilled. He could not explain how it had happened. No one had been in the bathroom.

Some of the Hermann's relatives also had strange experiences. A cousin of Mr. Hermann saw a small statue move around a table. Then it flew two feet into the air and landed on the rug.

Some of the bottles were taken to the police laboratory. The electric company checked the house to see if there was anything wrong with the electricity. Building inspectors and the fire department also examined the house. Everything about it seemed normal. They could find nothing to account for the disturbances.

The Hermann family was very upset by these goings-on. They appealed to the public for help. Naturally, the appeal got into the newspapers. The Long Island poltergeist became famous.

News of the poltergeist reached Dr. J.G. Pratt in North Carolina. Dr. Pratt is one of America's leading researchers on the subject of hauntings, ghosts, and other unexplained events.

He came up to Long Island to investigate the case in person. He interviewed everyone connected with the case. He checked over the house, and examined all the objects that had been disturbed.

By the time Dr. Pratt arrived, the disturbances

had died down considerably. He did not see any objects fly across the room. He did hear a few strange thumps coming from Jimmy's room. He was not able to come up with any explanation for the case. He left just as puzzled as he was when he came. The case has never been solved.

The most important poltergeist case in history also took place in America. It happened in the little town of Hydesville in Upstate New York. In March, 1848, strange noises were heard in the small house occupied by the blacksmith, John D. Fox, and his family. The noises came from the bedroom used by two of his daughters. The daughters were Margaret, or Maggie, who was fifteen years old, and Kate, or Katie, who was not quite twelve.

The noises were strange thumps or bumps. No one in the Fox family could explain what caused them. The Fox family told their neighbors about the noises. When neighbors visited, they heard the thumps too. Word spread quickly. People came from miles around to witness the strange events. The little town had never seen such excitement before.

The Fox sisters said they could "talk" to the spirit that was making noises.

Soon Kate and Maggie claimed that they could "talk" to the mysterious spirit that was making the noises. They used a sort of code. Someone would ask a question. The spirit would answer with signals—one rap if the answer was no, two if the answer was yes.

The boy in Washington was "cured" by an exorcism. The Long Island poltergeist just faded away. But interest in the strange noises that afflicted the Fox sisters continued to grow. The two girls soon began to "talk" to spirits more

103

directly. They became the first "spirit mediums." The rappings at Hydesville were the starting point for the movement called "spiritualism." Spiritualists believe that people can communicate with the dead with the aid of mediums. Within a few years people all over the world were communicating with spirits in different ways.

Basically, all three of these cases began the same way. A house was afflicted with strange noises. These noises centered around a child or teen-ager. Different people reacted in different ways. In one case, the noises were blamed on a demon. In another, on a spirit. Many psychical researchers do not think spirits or demons are the cause of poltergeist activity. They think that the cause may be some sort of unknown force. This force seems somehow to radiate from certain children.

Then there are those who believe that there is nothing supernatural about poltergeists at all. They think that natural explanations can be found. Usually the explanation is a child who is playing tricks on his or her parents. Often the child simply wants to attract attention.

In many poltergeist cases the children have actually been caught making the noises or shaking the bed. In other cases they have not been caught, but have confessed that is what they did.

Years after they became famous, the Fox sisters confessed that they had faked the noises when they were children. They had just wanted to play a trick on their mother. They got so much attention that they kept on playing tricks. Finally, so many people believed them that they felt they could not stop.

Later still, Maggie Fox took back her confession. She said she had not played any tricks at all. But most people today think that she did. Even people who believe in ghosts and spirits are very suspicious of the Fox sisters.

Could parents and other adults be fooled? Sure, they could. One of the main reasons they can be fooled is because they think that they can't. If they can't see the trickery they assume no one else can either, and that there is no trickery.

The Long Island poltergeist case provides a good example. A professional magician read accounts of the case. He said he thought he knew how some of the strange effects had been made.

The odd thing that happened most often was that bottles opened and spilled by themselves. What may have really happened, according to the magician, was this: The bottles were opened and spilled while no one was looking. Then when other people were around, the person who was playing the trick made a noise. Perhaps he hit the bottom of his chair, but no one saw him do it. Then he looked toward the place where the spilled bottles were. When the others found the opened bottles, they assumed that the noise had been made by the bottles. In fact, the noise and the bottles had nothing to do with one another. That is the sort of deception that magicians use on the stage all the time.

The magician also suggested other ways some of the strange incidents could be produced by trickery. He wanted to investigate the Hermann house. Mr. Hermann had allowed policemen, psychical researchers, newspapermen, and many others into his house. But he would not let the magician in. He was insulted because of the suggestion that his son was fooling him.

But no one could fake all the things a poltergeist is reported to do. For example, in some poltergeist cases objects are supposed to float in midair. But did things happen exactly as they were reported? People don't always see what they think they see. Often people forget some little detail. But details can be important. Usually a witness in a poltergeist case is upset. Sometimes he is frightened. When a person is in that condition he does not make the best witness.

People who believe in poltergeists admit that mistakes can be and have been made. But they don't think mistakes can explain all of the cases that they have collected over the years. They say there is something else as well.

8

INTO THE PAST

Did you ever get the feeling that you could step into the past? Maybe you felt that way when visiting some historic place. Of course, it is only a passing feeling. You are still firmly in the present.

But what if you looked up and suddenly found yourself surrounded by people dressed in the clothes of a different time?

This has happened to some people, at various places. The most impressive case took place in France at Versailles, once the palace of the French kings. In fact, it has happened several times at Versailles.

The first, and most important case, began on

Marie Antoinette

the afternoon of August 10, 1901. Two school-teachers were visiting France. Their names were Ann Mobery and Eleanor Jourdain. Miss Mobery was fifty-five years of age; Miss Jourdain was thirty-eight. Like most tourists in France, they came to Versailles. At that time they had no special interest in Versailles. Miss Jourdain had spent considerable time in France and spoke

French well, but had never been to Versailles.

The two women were just ordinary tourists following the directions in a popular guidebook. They were walking around the grounds of the huge palace trying to find a building called the Petit Trianon. It is a small palace near the larger main palace. This building had once been a favorite spot for Queen Marie Antoinette. She was the queen who was beheaded during the French Revolution.

The two women did not quite know where they were. Despite the instructions in the guidebook, they felt lost. As they walked through a small gate, things around them began to change. They saw what looked like empty farm buildings. Various farm tools were lying about. Everything looked deserted. The scene was very depressing.

As they walked on they felt stranger and stranger. It was as if they were walking in a dream. The buildings around looked like part of a stage set. They saw two men wearing long green coats and small three-cornered hats that looked like official uniforms. The two men told them to go straight on.

The farther the two schoolteachers walked, the more convinced they became that something was wrong. But each had this feeling independently. They said nothing to one another. They saw a dark-skinned, pock-marked man with a wide-brimmed hat and heavy cloak. His face looked "very evil." They were almost afraid to walk past him. Another man with a large hat and scarf shouted, "Ladies, you mustn't go that way. Go this way to look for the house."

Following the directions, they found the house and saw "a young girl standing in a doorway, who wore a white kerchief and dress to her ankles." There was another lady in a large hat and old-fashioned dress drawing a picture. When they came to another house a young man offered to take them around to the front. After he left them everything seemed to return to normal.

For some reason neither woman told the other for a week what she had seen or felt during the visit. In fact, they had almost forgotten about the strange experience. Only when one of them began to write a letter home did she begin to realize what had happened. She turned to her

The Petit Trianon

companion and said: "Do you think that the Petit Trianon is haunted?"

"Yes, I do," was the reply.

The two women agreed not to talk about what had happened any more. They wrote down separate versions of what they had experienced. They did not want to influence the other's memories. When they compared the two versions, they were very similar. They then decided that something strange and ghostly had happened on their visit to Versailles.

When she got back to England, Miss Jourdain talked to a Frenchwoman who worked at her school. She asked if there were any stories about the Petit Trianon being haunted. Miss Jourdain did not mention what had happened to her and her friend.

She was told there was a legend that regularly, on a certain day in August, Marie Antoinette could be seen outside the Petit Trianon. She was wearing a pink dress and a light flapping hat. This matched the figure they had seen sketching. Not only that, said the Frenchwoman, the whole Trianon area, "especially the farm, the garden, and the path by the water is peopled with those who used to be with her [Marie Antoinette] there." For a day and a night the area was supposed to be thrown back into the past. Of course, the Frenchwoman added, it is only a legend.

But legend or not, it confirmed the growing belief of Miss Mobery and Miss Jourdain that they had stepped into the past. For the next two years they did a lot of research on Versailles. They decided that they had stepped back into August 5, 1789. This was shortly before a mob

Marie Antoinette shortly before her execution.

from Paris marched on Versailles. By the end of 1789, both King Louis XVI and his queen, Marie Antoinette, were virtual prisoners. Both were executed in October, 1793.

With the aid of old maps and documents, Miss Mobery and Miss Jourdain thought they could trace exactly where they had walked. They even thought they could identify the dark-skinned, pock-marked man. They said he was the Comte de Vaudreuil, who had been born in the French colonies in America. De Vaudreuil was a friend of the queen's and was often at Versailles.

Eleanor Jourdain visited Versailles again in January, 1902. It was a cold wet day. As she walked near the Petit Trianon she was again overcome by a feeling of depression and strangeness. She became confused and lost her way. But she did not see any figures in old-fashioned clothes this time.

On July 4, 1904, three years after their strange adventure, both women again visited Versailles. Nothing was the same this time. A small building they had seen in 1901 was not there. There was a gravel path instead of a shaded meadow. A large bush grew where the lady in the large hat and long dress had been sketching. People walked wherever they wanted. No one showed them the way.

The two women wrote a book about their experience. The book was called *An Adventure.* It was quite popular. Many people talked to Eleanor Jourdain and Anne Mobery. Everyone who did was impressed by them. They were intelligent, reliable people. They didn't try to make money from their experience. They didn't want to become famous. They didn't even use their own names when they wrote.

There is no solid evidence to back up the story of the two witnesses. We have to take their word for what they say. But they are the best sort of witnesses. There is no reason to believe that they lied.

Could they have been mistaken? Some people think so. An English psychical researcher named R.J. Sturge-Whiting tried to reconstruct the whole case. He concluded that everything the two women saw was at Versailles at the time they visited it in 1901. The people they had seen were gardeners, amateur artists, and ordinary tourists. We must remember that the clothes of 1901 were not so different from those of 1789. There is a much bigger difference between the clothes of 1901 and those of today. No one could honestly mistake a modern tourist for someone in Marie Antionette's court. In 1901, such a mistake might have been possible, according to Sturge-Whiting.

A psychologist named Joseph Jastrow also studied the case. He suggests this "visit to the past" was really the result of wishful thinking. He imagined the two women walking through the palace gardens thinking, "Wouldn't it be thrilling to see Versailles as it was in Marie Antoinette's day!" In this instance, no sooner thought than seen.

There is no way of proving that the skeptics like Sturge-Whiting and Jastrow are right. But there is no way of proving they are wrong either.

As we said, the book the two Englishwomen wrote was very popular. Thousands of tourists have walked through the grounds of Versailles with a copy of *An Adventure* under their arm. Many wished they would have a similar adventure. Some said they did.

An Adventure was published in 1911. A few years later the Misses Mobery and Jourdain were contacted by a Mr. John Crooke. He said that from the year 1907 to 1909 he and his wife and son had lived in a flat overlooking the park at Versailles. On several occasions they saw people wearing what seemed like the clothes of another time. Once they saw a woman sketching. She looked very much like the woman described in *An Adventure.* But the family insisted they had their adventures before they read *An Adventure.* They said that they could not have been influenced by the book.

Two other English schoolteachers were walking through the Versailles gardens in 1928. Near the Petit Trianon they were suddenly overcome by a feeling of depression. They saw an old man in an old-fashioned green uniform coming toward them. He looked sinister. They tried to run away from him. But when they turned around he was gone. They described the experience to friends. One sent them a copy of *An Adventure.* The two women were amazed at how similar the experiences had been to those described in the book.

Ten years later, in 1938, Mrs. Elizabeth Hatton was walking down an avenue near the Petit Trianon. In front of her she saw a man and a woman in what looked like old-fashioned peasant dress. Marie Antoinette and some of her friends used to dress up as peasants at times. They often wore such costumes at the Petit Trianon. Mrs. Hatton said she never read *An Adventure* until after she had her experience.

In 1949, Jack Wilkinson, a British poultry

farmer, his wife and four-year-old son were strolling in the park at Versailles. They saw a woman wearing a long dress and carrying a parasol. These clothes were completely out of place in 1949. Wilkinson said when he first saw her he thought she was "a nut case." He didn't know how she could walk around like that without attracting attention.

The family watched the strange woman for a couple of minutes. But they didn't want to seem as if they were staring, though, of course, that is what they were doing. They turned away for a moment; when they turned back the woman was gone. She had disappeared. Wilkinson insists there was no way the woman could have gone into some hiding place. There were no buildings around. There were no trees or bushes to hide behind. She had just vanished.

A London lawyer and his wife had an adventure of their own at Versailles on May 21, 1955. A report of their experience was sent to the Society for Psychical Research. But the couple did not want publicity. The story was published without names.

They were walking down a path when they saw

two men and a woman coming toward them. The men were dressed all in black. They had black coats, black breeches, black stockings, and black shoes with silver buckles. The woman was wearing a bright yellow dress with a very full skirt that reached to the ground. It was the sort of outfit that might have been worn by people in the time of Marie Antoinette.

The lawyer and his wife wanted to get a closer look. But before they could get too near, the strange trio vanished. The lawyer and his wife could not account for the disappearance. The lawyer said that he had read *An Adventure* the year before his trip to Versailles. It is not known whether his wife read it or discussed it with him.

These are just some of the "adventures" reported at Versailles. Many others have been recorded by psychical researchers. Still more have probably never been written down at all.

Is Versailles—particularly the Petit Trianon— haunted? Does the area have some strange power to occasionally give people glimpses of what happened there hundreds of years ago? Is the woman in the long dress, who is so often "seen" during these experiences, the spirit of the tragic Queen?

It would certainly be exciting to answer yes to all of these questions.

But it is also possible that all of these experiences are the result of overactive imaginations. Many people said they had not read *An Adventure* until after their own experience. It is still possible that they had heard of the book, even if they did not remember it. They may have been ready to see the ghost of Marie Antoinette. Any person wearing an odd old-fashioned looking outfit could have triggered the experience. An imagination ready to go back to the past would have done the rest.

As I said, that could explain all the experiences. But on the other hand . . .

INDEX

124

About the Author

DANIEL COHEN is a free-lance writer and former managing editor of *Science Digest* magazine. He has written numerous books for adults and young readers on subjects ranging from science to the supernatural. Previous titles include *The Mysteries of Reincarnation, In Search of Ghosts, The Magic Art of Foreseeing the Future,* and *Mysterious Disappearances.* As high interest, low vocabulary books, he has prepared *The Greatest Monsters in the World* and *Supermonsters*. He also appears frequently on radio and television and has lectured at colleges and universities throughout the country.

Mr. Cohen is a native of Chicago and holds a degree in journalism from the University of Illinois. He lives with his wife, who is also a writer, their daughter, and a collection of cats and dogs in Port Jervis, New York.

j APR 1978   5

133.1
C   COHEN
         REAL GHOSTS

3 2395 00028 2745